D0066191

Safe Enough Spaces

Also by Michael S. Roth

Beyond the University: Why Liberal Education Matters

Memory, Trauma, and History: Essays on Living with the Past

Irresistible Decay: Ruins Reclaimed, with Clare Lyons and Charles Merewether

Freud: Conflict and Culture, Essays on His Life, Work and Legacy, editor

The Ironist's Cage: Trauma, Memory and the Construction of History

Disturbing Remains: Memory, History and Crisis in the Twentieth Century, coeditor with Charles G. Salas

Looking for Los Angeles: Architecture, Film, Photography and the Urban Landscape, coeditor with Charles G. Salas

History And...: Histories Within the Human Sciences, coeditor with Ralph Cohen

Rediscovering History: Culture, Politics and the Psyche, editor

Knowing and History: Appropriations of Hegel in Twentieth-Century France

Psycho-Analysis as History: Negation and Freedom in Freud

Safe Enough Spaces

*A Pragmatist's Approach to Inclusion,
Free Speech, and Political Correctness
on College Campuses*

MICHAEL S. ROTH

Yale UNIVERSITY PRESS

New Haven and London

Published with assistance from the foundation established in memory of Amasa Stone Mather of the Class of 1907, Yale College.

Copyright © 2019 by Michael S. Roth.
All rights reserved.
This book may not be reproduced, in whole or in part, including illustrations, in any form (beyond that copying permitted by Sections 107 and 108 of the U.S. Copyright Law and except by reviewers for the public press), without written permission from the publishers.

Yale University Press books may be purchased in quantity for educational, business, or promotional use. For information, please e-mail sales.press@yale.edu (U.S. office) or sales@yaleup.co.uk (U.K. office).

Set in Minion type by Integrated Publishing Solutions.
Printed in the United States of America.

Library of Congress Control Number: 2019931177

ISBN 978-0-300-23485-5 (hardcover : alk. paper)

A catalogue record for this book is available from the British Library.

This paper meets the requirements of ANSI/NISO Z39.48-1992 (Permanence of Paper).

10 9 8 7 6 5 4 3 2 1

For Wesleyan University

Contents

Preface and Acknowledgments

I've been teaching college students since 1983, first at Scripps College and then at the Claremont Graduate University, UCLA, the California College of the Arts, and, for the last decade or so, at Wesleyan University, where I myself was an undergrad in the mid-1970s. For almost twenty years, I have combined that teaching with administrative work, mostly as a college president. I have a Ph.D. in history but have never been very happy staying within a single department. As an undergraduate, I was able to create my own major (history of psychological theory), and at Scripps College I jumped at the opportunity to found a Humanities Institute and offer classes across a range of fields. I later had the good fortune to run the international scholars program at the Getty Research Institute, in which artists and scholars from different disciplines come together to work on projects related to a common theme. Intellectual diversity has inspired and sustained me, mostly because I have always been eager to learn—and needed to learn—from scholars whose preparation and interests are very different from my own.

Intellectual diversity, I have found, is most effective if it complements other modes of difference within an academic community. Racial, ethnic, religious, and economic diversities on campus increase the likelihood that students and teachers will hear different points of view, encounter a variety of experiences, and forge more inclusive projects as they connect campus learning to life beyond the university. Of course, the fact that one belongs to a specific demographic group doesn't necessarily mean one will have a particular point of view, and campuses can become balkanized into separate silos based on identity or politics. But bringing to a campus students from diverse backgrounds, with a variety of ideas, creates more possibilities for learning from people different from oneself.

As president of the university, I am often the one students turn to when they find unhappy differences—say, between their political or moral values and what they perceive to be the direction of the school. We find ways to discuss these conflicts, not usually with the expectation that we will land on consensus, but in order to acknowledge and clarify where we disagree and where we might continue to learn from each other (or work toward a common goal). At Wesleyan and at other universities, tensions on some issues don't typically derail finding common purpose on other ones. Faculty, staff, or students who might be quite sure of their antagonistic positions on an educational policy matter find ways to reason together to make progress on other issues. Of course, sometimes the tensions or the differences are too great and productive conversation breaks down. These days when that happens, especially when groups of students are involved, there is almost always someone there with a phone to video the mess. But most of the time it's not like that. Members of the campus community are used to intellectual conflict—inside and outside the classroom—and this often means leaving their comfort zones, hearing perspectives they didn't expect to hear. And most campuses are "safe enough" for that to happen.

The phrase "safe enough" recalls the "good enough" parenting concept of the British psychoanalyst D. W. Winnicott. A good-enough parent enables a child to flourish, whereas a parent aiming to be perfect (to orchestrate an ideal childhood) winds up creating immense difficulties for a youngster needing to experience failure in order to grow. As a teacher and university president, I find that schools that promote a basic sense of inclusion and respect enable students to flourish—to be open to ideas and perspectives so that the differences they encounter are educative. That basic sense is feeling "safe enough."

❖

A number of the arguments here were developed in opinion pieces, blog posts, and book reviews that I've written over the past few years. I am grateful to the *Washington Post,* the *New York Times,* the *Wall Street Journal, Inside Higher Education,* and the *Chronicle of Higher Education* for the opportunities to publish in their pages. Peter Dougherty, an editor at Princeton University Press, discussed the germ of the idea for this book, and Jennifer Banks and her team at Yale University Press, especially the manuscript editor, Julie Carlson, have been thoughtful and attentive in seeing the project through. With respect to preparing the manuscript of this book, my former student, longtime colleague, and old friend Charles Salas has helpfully provided notes on what I've written (and, sometimes, what I should have written). I am grateful to them all.

Wesleyan University is known for its engaged student body, its emphasis on interdisciplinarity and critical thinking, and its dedication to providing an "education in the liberal arts that is characterized by boldness, rigor, and practical idealism." As an undergraduate there in the 1970s, I critically engaged with its policies and administration even as I was transformed by its enlivening faculty and campus culture. Now during my tenure as president, the university community has been generous with its (varied and ample!) criticism of my views. Exploring the ramifications of pragmatic liberal education in particular, and the issues facing higher education in general, is at once my responsibility as a college president, and a passionate research interest. In this, my engagement with the extraordinary students, faculty, staff, and alumni of Wesleyan University has been and continues to be essential to my thinking and my writing. I dedicate this book to them.

I wrote most of this book sitting across the room (or just a table) from my wife, Kari Weil, as she worked on her own scholarly projects. For more than twenty years now, the spaces we've created have certainly been safe enough. She continues to teach me how to avoid getting stuck in comfort zones, how to learn from different diversities, and how to find joy in mutual discovery and recognition.

Introduction

S uspicion about colleges and universities is nothing new. From their very beginnings, they have aroused curiosity and attracted critique. Is the education that students get really worthwhile? Is it relevant to the world beyond the halls of study? If students emerge from those halls changed, are those changes for the better? And who decides what "better" means? Those who taught them? Those who welcome them back home? Those who hire them? In the medieval period, universities were charged with regulating religious authority, and they were sometimes torn by theological debates or by tensions between students and teachers. Later, Thomas Hobbes blamed the English Civil War on republicans led astray at universities by the ideas of the ancient Greeks and Romans, concluding that "the Universities have been to the nation, as the wooden horse was to the Trojans." Hobbes wanted the sovereign power to take control of education to ensure sound morals and civil obedience, for only then could there be consensus and thus peace. Republican revolutionary and American president Thomas Jefferson, who founded the University of Virginia, was chagrined near the end of his life to find that student culture was not easily controlled, whether the undergrads were demanding new fields of study or just rabble rousing on the quad and harassing "European" faculty. "Coercion must be resorted to," he lamented, "where confidence has been disappointed."[1]

Has confidence in universities today been disappointed? Is coercion on the way? As I write this in the fall of 2018, the Trump administration is weighing in against colleges using race in admissions decisions, and several states are considering legislation that would insist schools teach in a certain way, or that they modify their procedures for inviting lecturers to campus.

This is a crucial time for higher education in America. It is an era of enormous achievement and promise, but also great uncertainty and danger. In some ways, the vitality of our strongest institutions has never been more apparent. American research universities dominate the lists of the world's best, and students from across the globe have for many years seen our country as the best place to pursue post-secondary learning. But that may be changing, and here at home things have already changed. In recent years, colleges have been increasingly viewed with suspicion, and sometimes outright hostility. Institutions of higher learning are facing enormous pressures to demonstrate the cash value of their "product," while at the same time the recreational side of campus life is attracting more attention than ever. To meet enrollment goals or climb in the rankings, many colleges trumpet the "full spa experience," placing more and more emphasis on the value of what young consumers are learning while enjoying themselves *outside* the classroom. The richness of the curriculum and high quality of the instruction may receive a nod, but they are rarely celebrated. These efforts at promotion through everything *ex-*

elementary and high schools, and that it is increasingly difficult for low-income families to find educational opportunities
that will result in them being college-ready at age seventeen.
Richard V. Reeves has described "opportunity hoarding" by
the wealthiest fifth of the American population. The upper-
middle class has focused on securing special privileges for its
children, he writes, adding that "education has . . . become the
main mechanism for the reproduction of upper-middle class
status across generations."[18] As inequality has gotten worse, the
benefits of having a college diploma have gotten greater. Still,
at many elite schools we continue to privilege the privileged—
whether through admissions offices that give alumni relatives
an advantage, or through geographically based marketing plans
that aim recruiting messages at those already most likely to succeed because of the advantages they already have. The essential question is how American universities can provide more
opportunity for deep learning among the most disadvantaged
populations. What would it take for these schools to think of
this as a civic responsibility essential to their mission?

I emphasize colleges with high graduation rates because
recruiting students from these groups to schools from which
they are less likely to graduate is bad for them and bad for the
institutions. Schools with high graduation rates often have developed sophisticated student services departments, and they
are more likely to keep students from taking on excessive debt.
The gap between the numbers of poor and rich folks who attend college has shrunk, but the gap between poor and rich
who graduate college has grown. Far too many economically
disadvantaged students are finding their way to colleges only to
leave without a degree (and often with loans). They don't drop
out pleased to have taken some interesting classes; they leave

frustrated with higher education in general. It is not enough to open more widely the gates to the university; there must be programs on every campus to inspire all students to succeed on campus and beyond the university.

❖

In 2017–2018, an academic year of intense controversies concerning race and class on college campuses across the country, a Harvard University task force published *Pursuing Excellence on a Foundation of Inclusion*.[19] The report aimed to help move the university beyond increasing diversity and toward equity and inclusion in hiring and admissions, teaching and social life, working conditions for staff, and the process of curriculum development. Variations on the word "flourish" appear at least eighteen times in the glossy eighty pages. Affirmative action is mentioned only once—in the context of reports required for compliance purposes.

The report does early on note the importance of "deliberate attention and effort" for achieving diversity in various endeavors and the necessity of overcoming biases in any particular selection process (such as admissions or hiring). But expanding access is no longer at the top of the agenda. That place belongs to inclusion:

> The intellectual fruits of a community's inner diversity do not harvest themselves. To gain the benefit of diversity, Harvard must fully integrate all members of the University into academic, professional, and social contexts that support their individual flourishing and activate their potential. Excellence requires successful practices of inclusion at all levels, from the interpersonal to the organizational.[20]

The "benefits of full belonging" have replaced the more straightforward goal of increased access. Belonging involves not simply assimilation to the existing institutional culture, but also a sense of being included in the active molding of that culture's evolution. At Harvard, it also means that people from previously under-represented groups who have earned access to the university should have the chance to thrive—to fulfill their potential. "When students, staff, faculty members, or academic personnel are integrated into our community in ways that permit them to do their best work, we anticipate that they will experience a sense of full belonging." The task force is confident that individuals can achieve a "sense of full belonging" and "do their best work" without having to give up their particular community affiliations. In other words, belonging isn't reducible to successful assimilation to mainstream Harvard culture. You can stay true to your particular group and still belong to the university as a whole. There is confidence that loyalty to the practices of your own group will still allow you (maybe even empower you) to do your best work in the context of the university community.

The authors of *Pursuing Excellence on a Foundation of Inclusion* are aware of the challenges of measuring (or even understanding) what counts as a person's best work, and they well know how a sense of belonging can be shaken by argument, controversy, and the kind of criticism that is at the heart of an academic institution. Simply put, teachers can more easily cultivate belonging in their classrooms if they keep all the students happy, if they don't ask them to leave their comfort zones. Giving most students an "A" or "A−" seems to have become a baseline of inclusion at many very selective schools across the country. For what would happen when you learn that your idea is wrong, or that your experimental design is flawed, or that your conclusion doesn't follow from your evidence and argument? Would you still feel you belong? Would you still feel you are flourishing?

The Harvard task force members address these issues through the lens of academic freedom, by which they mean, in part, the freedom to tell someone that her or his idea is wrongheaded. They take as absolutely essential the university's commitment to protect free inquiry and the ability to express one's academic/professional views without fear of social or political punishment. They reject the notion that there is a necessary conflict between the value of this freedom and the desire to cultivate the value of inclusion—claiming instead that these values "provide each other with synergistic and mutual reinforcement."[21] After all, academic freedom would be an empty concept if everyone started with a similar set of ideas, if there was no diversity of viewpoints to protect. And inclusion would be meaningless at a university if it meant there were no attempts to cultivate excellence along with belonging; people may feel they belong to a resort community by virtue of using its facilities, but a university community demands intellectual growth from its members, and this process can be, should be, contentious. Despite the amenities arms race at many American schools, a university exists to instigate achievement and not just to offer the experience of a luxury spa. Academic achievement requires that bad ideas be rejected; it requires a critical attitude that exposes fallacious reasoning so as to arrive at better ways of thinking and acting. If one prioritizes inclusion, will this critical process take a back seat in favor of wanting people to feel at home in a community? The Harvard report answers "no" to this question: inclusion is joined to the idea of flourishing, of developing one's full potential. In an academic setting, this begins with the notion that heterodox viewpoints will be protected to the extent that they will be carefully, re-spectfully, considered. This consideration, however, doesn't mean that all ideas will be found to have equal merit—only that they will have an equal opportunity to be studied. The authors of the Harvard report recognize the challenges that follow from attempting to hold together rigorous inquiry and respectful belonging as core values, but they see this as fundamental to the future of the university. At Harvard, they want to create a culture that permits members "to be their authentic selves and that support[s] their academic and professional success, even while challenging them to grow."[22] It may well happen that one's sense of authenticity will be challenged by what one learns, making it harder to stay true to one's prior set of personal or communal allegiances. If part of one's identity, for example, is bound up with a community's rejection of modern medicine or the theory of evolution, then it will be harder to study the modern life sciences with the same sense of belonging that some other students enjoy. We might agree that the biology professor shouldn't merely mock these beliefs, but that instructor shouldn't have to dance around what they entail, either. There may be students who have been brought up to believe that vaccinations are forms of poison, but the professor can't spend too much time ensuring that they feel comfortable. The authors of the inclusion report use the idea of "academic freedom" as the foundation for the professor's responsibility to not change the biology course so as to be inoffensive to all students, but they also want all students to feel respected in that same class. Clearly, there will be some points of tension between helping students stay true to their authentic selves or their original communities and teaching our best ideas of what is true.

The political theorist Danielle Allen, one of the co-chairs

of the Harvard task force that produced the report, has written powerfully about all forms of education as aspiring "to direct the development of human capacities." No matter if it's vocational or liberal, she argues, the point of learning is to stimulate human flourishing, and a vital part of that flourishing is public life, the practices of citizenship. These practices demand a respect for differences; they require the ability to work through disagreements for the sake of communal goals. Allen underscores that education should cultivate "participatory readiness," and recognizes the necessity of political equality for enabling effective, responsible engagement in the public sphere.[23] A university community must confront the effects of inequality if it is to enable all its members to flourish, and if it is to enable meaningful political engagement.

Near the beginning of this century, Harvard set out to define its core values and concluded with four: respect, honesty, excellence, and accountability. The 2018 report on inclusion suggests adding a fifth: "Cultivate bonds and bridges that enable all to grow with and learn from one another."[24] Learning from one another across differences is not just transactional—it also depends on building ongoing relationships that foster belonging and inclusion—relationships that sustain community. Supporting those ideas while pursuing the contentious, sometimes antagonistic path of free inquiry is the challenge facing many colleges and universities today. It is the challenge of recognizing and respecting different forms of diversity and using them for their educational benefits. We both want the benefits of antagonism and need the benefits of cooperation.

Pursuing Excellence on a Foundation of Inclusion is a noble attempt to shift attention from admissions and access to harvesting the fruits of education. But admissions at Harvard has recently been thrust back into the spotlight thanks to the lawsuit concerning possible discrimination against Asian American applicants. The lawsuit has been brought by Students for Fair Admissions, led by Edward Blum, a tried and true enemy of affirmative action, and a new friend to this particular demographic group. For many years Blum has led litigation efforts animated by the principle, as he puts it, that "your race and your ethnicity should not be something used to help you or harm you in your life's endeavors."[25] He has attacked voting rights laws that, he thinks, attempt to elect candidates of a specific ethnic or racial group, and he has attacked educational diversity efforts that treat individuals differently because of the racial group with which they identify.

The litigation against Harvard is ongoing as I write, and in the summer of 2018 Blum's group began releasing documents aimed to show that the university's admissions policies are unfair to Asian Americans with strong test scores and grades. A white applicant with the same scores and grades would have, according to a Duke economist's analysis of the documents, a 10 percent greater chance of admission than an Asian American, and an African American a 75 percent greater chance. Published documents from the discovery phase of the litigation seem to show admissions officers using crude stereotyping of Asian Americans to justify not accepting people who are "too driven" by grades and test scores. These practices, too overt to be called "implicit bias," occur in the so-called personality score section of the admissions process. Usually, Blum's group argues, applicants with the strongest academic standing also do well on the personality score. But, they claim, an "Asian-American penalty" is imposed by admissions officers when they rank applicants. If the plaintiffs can demonstrate that the university has a separate system of admissions criteria for these students, they can show that the so-called holistic process is

just a cover for crude racial quotas. Such a quota would mean
that the so-called penalty on one minority group (Asian American applicants) is in place to create a "bonus" to benefit members of other minority groups (African American and Latinx
applicants). There are distinct tracks at many universities for
athletes, large donors, and alumni relatives. Blum's group is
focused on race but not on these traditional forms of affirmative action, which surely have resulted in fewer available slots
for the admission of students of color. "This lawsuit filed by
Edward Blum in the name of Asian-American students," de-
clared Jin Hee Lee, deputy director of litigation at the NAACP
Legal Defense and Educational Fund, "is a dangerous ploy to
distort the benefits of diversity for college students of all races,
despite settled law on this issue."[26] Nobody is fooled, and the
goal of the litigation is clear: dismantle the use of race in the
admissions process.

A group of distinguished research universities has filed
an amicus brief in the lawsuit, reminding the court of the def-
erence usually shown to academic institutions in regard to
how they determine the educational policies that guide them.
Admissions policies are a crucial facet of constructing a learning community, and ensuring a diverse student body is a fundamental aspect of that construction. "A student body that is
diverse in many dimensions," note the brief's authors, "including racial and ethnic background, produces enormous educational benefits." The schools go on to explain that to ignore
race as an essential part of a person's identity would signifi-
cantly undermine this process of creating diversity "in many
dimensions." The amicus brief rehearses the arguments from
earlier affirmative action cases that left room for universities to
determine how best to balance a variety of factors in creating
a vibrant and diverse student body. The universities point out

that in an increasingly polarized and segregated society, the campus provides a particularly important opportunity for people with different identities and different ideas to learn from one another. The rhetoric of inclusion may have become prevalent in on-campus discussions of diversity, but that's only in an environment where affirmative action in admissions is a protected practice. The Harvard litigation is a reminder that without access to people from a variety of backgrounds, inclusion is pretty meaningless.[27]

In his first year in office, President Trump announced that his administration would be joining in the lawsuit against Harvard University—clearly seeing the litigation as a vehicle for undermining affirmative action programs more generally. *The New York Times* reported that the White House wanted the U.S. Department of Justice to "redirect resources" of its civil rights division "toward investigating and suing universities over affirmative action admissions policies deemed to discriminate against white applicants."[28] Subsequently, the Department of Justice said that it was really just seeking "volunteers" interested in a lawsuit alleging discrimination against Asian Americans, but more recently the Trump administration made clear its interest in the case.

President Trump is clearly playing to his political base, for whom the only thing more popular than criticizing affirmative action would be attacking immigrants. Under the guise of protecting the rights of Asian Americans, the beleaguered attorney general Sessions played the role of defender of white people threatened by opportunities given to minorities. But apart from the cynical political opportunism of this move, we can also see the threats against affirmative action as another effort to use higher education to protect those who already have key social advantages. As of the fall of 2018, there has been no criticism from the White House of the university's policies that give preferences in admissions to athletes and the children of alumni and potential donors. These groups are predominantly white, though presumably many members of these groups don't think of their whiteness as a primary source of their identity.

In an admissions marketplace in which there are far more qualified applicants than there are available spots in a frosh class, conflicts concerning merit, social mobility, fairness, diversity, and group allegiance are bound to emerge. Ever since Socrates asked his young interlocutors to rethink their beliefs about justice and truth, education has exposed tension points between allegiance to some aspects of one's community and the practice of seeking better ways of thinking and living. It may be that the heightened visibility of some of these tensions today stems from the ways in which affirmative action and other recruiting practices that expanded access to universities created more numerous possibilities for conflicted allegiances. For decades American culture has been preaching the importance of identity validation, even if humanities professors press the point that identities are often a matter of improvisation and performance. Students from groups that have long been under-represented on a campus have been told that their authentic identities matter and that in their pursuit of an education they should be able to affirm them. For many, that's what flourishing means. When the path of affirmation collides with corrosively critical academic practices—or just with the ways of the academic tribe—conflicts break out. Although contemporary faculty do not often face the Athenian charge of corrupting the youth of the city, they may face accusations of not showing sufficient respect for, or not accommodating, the habits or practices that students from different backgrounds bring with them to the college campus.

The conversation concerning diversity in higher education is being impacted not only by campus tensions between cultures of identity affirmation and practices of critical inquiry, but also by the much broader phenomenon of accelerating inequalities in the United States. For the past thirty years or so, the incomes of most Americans have stalled, while a small percentage of families have seen dramatic increases in their wealth. Within this general pattern, over the past twenty years, the gap between low-income Americans and those at the median has not increased substantially, but the gap between the highest earners and those with median incomes has continued to expand. The wealthy are increasingly able to isolate themselves not only from the poor, but also from middle and moderately well-off Americans. "Income segregation," the tendency of social classes to cluster in specific residential areas, is rising along with economic inequality generally.[29] Money has long bought economic segregation, but until fairly recently in America this meant that rich people were separating themselves from the poor. Since the 1990s, however, the wealthy have also been purchasing distance from the lived concerns of middle and even upper-middle-class co-citizens. The implications of all this are, of course, enormous for college campuses. First, there is a basic sense in which rising inequality makes having a college diploma more important than ever. Although the cost of a college education for most has risen greatly over the past thirty years, the return on investment remains strong. The income premium that comes from having an undergraduate degree has grown even while wages in general have stagnated.[30] People without a college diploma are at a serious economic disadvantage.

So getting into college is an important tool for earning at least a reasonable income, and many low-income students continue to see it as an important ingredient for economic mobility. But most low-income students in higher education attend institutions with the lowest graduation rates, putting them at a distinct disadvantage in climbing toward or above the median income. At most selective colleges and universities, those from the bottom half of the economic ladder make up less than a third of the student body, and there is a sharply disproportionate representation of wealthy students. These undergrads sit in the same classes, eat in the same lunchrooms, and often live in the same residence halls. Campus may be the only place many have had contact with someone from an economic class so different from their own. There should be diversity benefits from this contact, but there are also tensions for these students around what it means to feel included and to be valued for one's authentic self. Flourishing can have different meanings when the students' starting points are so disparate.

Many schools today emphasize the recognition of low-income and "first-generation" students, but young people are put into a strange situation when they are asked to ground their authentic selves in these communities. When a student asked me about celebrating low-income culture as we celebrate, say, African American or Jewish culture on campus, we wound up having an intense discussion about his ambition to be far above the low-income bracket after graduation. At the same time, he wanted me to know, quite rightly, that he was not at all ashamed of being from a low-income family. Indeed, he was proud of his family and the sacrifices they had made so he could attend our university. But he also wanted me to know that he was determined to use his college education to earn more money and eventually support his mother. On the other side of the coin, a friend who is a university trustee confided to me his ambivalence about being singled out as a "first-gen" success story. His own children can't identify with him in this regard; by definition, they can't be first generation. What does it mean for them to have their own success stories on a diverse campus, he asked? Flourishing through education is clearly a complicated matter when one is supposed to be both open to change and proud of one's roots.

The challenges of fostering inclusion on diverse campuses are heightened by the dramatic inequalities off campus. Students take note when some of their classmates go off together on vacations at fancy ski resorts while others have to stay in dorms because they can't afford to go home—or even have no home to return to. Administrators and professors may tell those left behind that it is their good fortune to be able to stay on campus and study, but many of these young people may feel they are at a disadvantage when it comes to having the "full college experience."

In today's economy, the middle class is under increased pressure, and students thinking about their prospects are well aware they may wind up either a happy economic winner or a sorry loser. Many feel even more competitive economic pressure because they see so little space between being wildly successful and being a dismal failure. In an environment like this, students from under-represented groups may feel at a serious disadvantage vis-à-vis their wealthy peers when it comes to feeling included or flourishing. Even at schools that claim, as mine does, to meet the full economic need of any enrolled student, these undergraduates may find that just being admitted into the institution does not enable them to take full advantage of its resources. Yes, they can ask professors and classmates to "check their privilege"; yes, they can demand that their school provide resources for tutoring, psychological services, and community building. But wealthy students have networks for internships and job hunting that even the most resourceful career center will find challenging to replicate. Institutions that want to enhance belonging by overcoming privileges generally have hard choices to make in allocating resources. Devote more resources to bring in more low-income students? Or devote them to helping a smaller number of students truly flourish? If a selective private school has 20 percent Pell-eligible students, it might set a target of increasing financial aid resources so as to enroll 25 percent of these low-income folks in the future. Alternatively, with more resources, it can set the goals of providing greater academic and psychological support for the cohort already on campus. Most institutions find it difficult to do either, and very few can do both.[31]

❖

Wherever one stands on issues of affirmative action, most can agree that diversity isn't just about admissions—it's about the educational culture created by a university. There are different types of diversity, and they serve different purposes. As conversations about race and learning moved away from the emphasis on access through affirmative action, student groups and university administrators increasingly turned to complex issues of equity and inclusion. It wasn't enough to have demographic diversity—the appropriate numbers of students from different racial, ethnic, and income groups. How were representatives of these "under-represented groups" experiencing the "historically white" institutions in which they were enrolled? Did all members of the university community have equal opportunities to make use of the school's resources? How could the institution be a home for all of its students?

Access or inclusion? For the students already on campus, inclusion is the more relevant. But critics have wondered to what extent demands by students for full inclusion are really demands to stay in their comfort zones, to not be challenged by others. How has the desire for inclusion and flourishing been re-framed as a demand for political correctness? This is the subject of the next chapter.

2

The Use and Abuse
of Political Correctness

"The strange thing about Political Correctness is that it seems to have lots of opponents and no supporters," wrote Roger Ebert in his 1994 review of the film *PCU*. "No one ever describes themselves as PC, and yet somehow the movement thrives." Until very recently, one would have said that political correctness (by which I mean accusations of it) reached its heyday in the 1990s. Baby boomers complained that college campuses were leaving behind their anarchic Animal House ways and becoming too uptight and rigidly moralistic. National Lampoon's *Animal House* had been released in 1978 (the year I graduated from college), and the corrupt authority figure, Dean Wormer, was the unforgettable villain. But by the 1990s, it was not priggish establishment types like Wormer who were being portrayed as the enemies of liberty, pleasure, and free thinking on campus. It was the campus radicals; it was they who were cast as the new authoritarians, and their rejection of the status quo was recoded as a disguised conformism—that is, political correctness. After a hiatus in

which the label "PC" faded somewhat as a term of public deri-
sion, in the past five years or so it has returned, "bigly." Nothing seems easier for self-proclaimed individualists than joining
in with others who reject conformism; nothing unites people
quite like the moral disavowal of the priggishly politically correct. People in the United States and around the world regu-
larly bond together by denouncing groupthink. Donald Trump
realized the power of being anti-PC somewhere between his
guest appearances on the Howard Stern radio show and his
run for the presidency: no matter what he said or did, he could
take the high ground, or at least earn credit, for not being
politically correct. In one of the early debates in the 2016 election, Megyn Kelly questioned the candidate about his de-
meaning comments about women over the years. "I think the
big problem this country has is being politically correct," he
replied. Throughout the election, he turned what might have
been judged moral lapses into heroic refusals to conform to
politically correct moral criteria. Other candidates have now
learned this lesson, especially, but not exclusively, on the Right.
As Ebert put it, "Nothing creates quite such a warm inner glow
as accusing others of being morally reprehensible." If PC police
are presumed to know the warmth of that feeling, those who
attack them surely do as well.[1]

Ebert was right to point out that in his day nobody admitted to wanting the label "politically correct," but this hasn't
always been the case. In the period between the two world
wars, the words were used to describe whether a particular
political action or policy was in line with a general theory—
usually Marxist or Communist theory. So, for example, a group
of farmers might go on strike over unfair wages (or prices for
their produce), and the party ideologues would debate whether

this labor action was really in accord with the party's general pronouncements on rural labor, political action, and the eventual destruction of capitalism. The tactic of getting farmers to support a strike might seem effective, but if in some way it was out of step with party goals, it would not be politically correct.[2]

It wasn't long before the term "politically correct" acquired pejorative connotations meant to call out those who refused to deviate from what was judged to be mindless orthodoxy. When Stalin decided to sign the non-aggression pact with Hitler, "correct" communists supported that decision despite having claimed for years that the Nazi leader was evil. Those on the Left who were dumbfounded by this alliance— like those who would later find party decisions (or murderous actions) corrupt and reprehensible—labeled their former comrades "politically correct" in this negative sense: in sync with official doctrine but out of touch with the moral basis of politics and the real world.[3]

Among those who identified with the Left in the late 1960s, there were some who fooled themselves into thinking they were at once nonconformists and also politically correct. Not the unrepentant Stalinists, who after the 1950s would probably not have viewed nonconformity as anything particularly positive. It was young Leftists in the West who had turned from Russia to China for inspiration, coating their ignorance with enthusiasm. For Americans wanting a taste of Chairman Mao's wisdom, the English translation of *The Little Red Book* provided positive uses of being "correct" in a political sense. As literary scholar Ruth Perry has noted, Mao's essay "On the Correct Handling of Contradictions among the People" was widely read by leftist intellectuals, and in it the chairman recommended kinder, gentler ways of resolving political tensions (such as discussion and critical thinking) than those he practiced (leading to the deaths of millions).[4] Cryptic sayings like "let a hundred flowers bloom" inspired some readers to find a radical politics that would be *correctly* in sync with the leader's view of history and the possibilities for revolution. At the same time, Maoism was just one movement within the New Left. More broadly, the anti-doctrinaire aspects of 1960s radicalism eschewed any question of alignment with theory, any effort to be "correct." Across the country, a youth culture developed on college campuses that opposed the deplorable war in Vietnam, dismissed establishment rules that protected racial and gender inequality, and was generally suspicious of the mores of adults. Theodore Roszak, in a prescient essay published in 1968, cast blame on the older generations for their failure to address any of the issues that were animating the concerns of the young. The adult generation, he wrote, "has surrendered its responsibility to make morally demanding decisions, to generate ideals, to control public authority, to safeguard the life of the community against its despoilers." The counterculture, as Roszak dubbed the "great refusal" of the young, didn't have a theoretical politics according to which it could be "correct." It had a target to reject: the world of alienation, violence, and inequality in which the young were being asked to take part.[5] Critics of this youth culture dismissed it using the sort of psychological reductionism we find in recent critiques of campus intolerance and political correctness. The conservative religious pundit Norman Vincent Peale, for example, wrote that "the U.S. was paying the price of two generations that followed the Dr. Spock baby plan of instant gratification of needs"; and Vice President Spiro Agnew chimed in, blaming Spock for the "permissiveness" that had led to spirited, radical disorder. These infantile explanations were embraced on the Right, and conservative adults scornfully labeled student protestors "the Spock generation."[6]

Members of this generation who saw themselves as countercultural struggled with how aligned with one another they should be as they pushed back against the mainstream that they criticized for demanding conformity. Did the radical opposition have to be united, or was that just a symptom of the conformism against which it was fighting? In looking at how the term "politically correct" was used in feminist circles, Ruth Perry takes note of a gentle dispute between two writers and activists, Toni Cade Bambara and Audre Lorde, friends in the late 1970s. Bambara had described herself (in a Notes to Contributors) as "a young Black woman who writes, teaches, organizes, lectures, tries to learn and tries to raise her daughter to be a correct little sister." Some months later, Lorde responded with a poem entitled "Dear Toni Instead of a Letter of Congratulation upon Your Book and Your Daughter Whom You Say You Are Raising to Be a Correct Little Sister." Not many brief bios have inspired such poetry, and Lorde's generous, moving lines about mothering daughters get at the disquiet of that time about being "in sync" with any doctrine, political or otherwise:

> As she moves through taboos
> Whirling myths like gay hoops over her head
> I know beyond fear and history
> That our teaching means keeping trust
> With less and less correctness
> Only with ourselves

Lorde is offering a loving reminder to her friend that their daughters don't have to "handle contradictions" correctly, and that they can find their own paths.